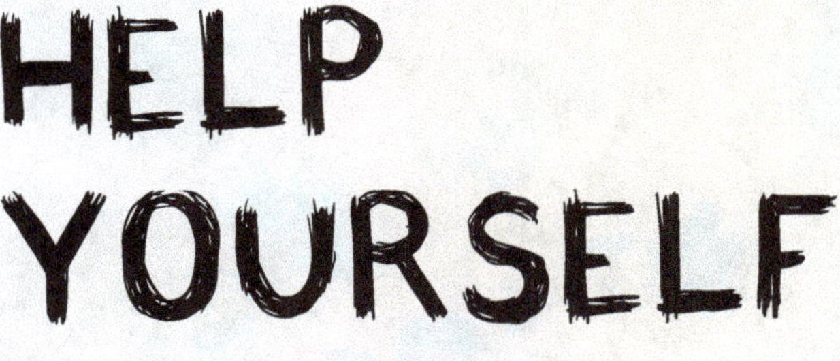

HELP YOURSELF

to some

TATIANA MININA

To the most wonderful
person in the world.
You are loved.
You are amazing.
Be happy!

First things first:
I'm not a therapist.
I won't unpack your traumas or help you navigate your feelings, at least not directly. And I don't want to see you in my office on a weekly basis.

Don't take me wrong, if you are going through a major life crisis or are experiencing mental health symptoms that affect your quality of life, counseling might be a great choice for you.

My goal here is to coax you out of your comfort zone and into happier pastures. I will help you feel better, switch off the autopilot, and enjoy your life a bit more.

This workbook is designed to nudge you in the right direction, improve your mood, and help you grow. It will open your eyes and ears to the simple yet unexpected experience of truly loving and accepting yourself.

ACT
NOW!

WHAT IF

you stopped delaying your life?

How often do you tell yourself " I'll do this or that once I finish with work, chores, or errands." How often do you find yourself not doing that thing you wanted to do, or when you did the experience was nowhere near as enjoyable as you anticipated?

The culprit is that you've spent hours, days, or even months dreaming, planning, and imagining the event, so by the time it actually takes place in real life, your brain feels as if it has already lived through it.

You may have noticed a similar pattern with your goals, You plan and strategize to achieve something, envisioning the result, but once you start putting your plan into action, more often than not, you lose interest and soon give up.

So how can you improve?

If possible, do things that make you happy sooner than later,
Don't dwell on them, and don't think about them too much. Allow
yourself to have a pure experience that you can later recall as a
memory.

If you want to achieve a goal, start taking steps right away.
Create an overall plan and define the end result, but don't
overthink it, and don't live through it in your mind.
I'm not suggesting you avoid careful planning, but rather modify
it and break it down into shorter, well-researched, and
immediately actionable steps.

There is no such thing as perfect timing other than here and
now. However, being "here and now", is not something most of us
are used to.
Here is a simple exercise to help you connect with the current
moment and unplug from the white noise of overthinking.

Take 2 minutes and write down:

Right now

I hear...

I see...

I feel,...

You will realize that it is not as easy as it seems. Your thoughts will constantly drift to unrelated things, and you will catch your mind trying to make conclusions from imaginary chains of events. This is perfectly normal. Note these thoughts, acknowledge them, and agree with them if needed. I often go with, 'Okay, but here and now...'

My other secret is a simple twenty-minute walk in the morning. Dear runners, please don't judge me, I'm not against running, but for this purpose, a walk is what we need, and a slow one at that. You can either listen to your favorite music or enjoy the sound of your surroundings, but the goal is to avoid planning and thinking about your day and instead focus on noticing every detail around you.

Once you connect to the "here and now" you notice that life becomes more enjoyable, and it becomes easier to make choices that are beneficial to you.

THE SECRET

of being in the flow.

The concept of being "in the flow" is often mentioned these days. Psychologists, coaches, and influencers all talk about it, but what does it really mean? How can you achieve this state of being fully immersed and engaged? While you may come across advice like unplugging from social media, finding pleasure in activities, enjoying the journey, being present, and avoiding negative thoughts, these are actually the outcomes of being in the flow rather than the means to get there. So, what should you do?

The flow is all about energy. When you lack energy, you're not in the flow. The key lies in conserving your energy by not wasting it on worries and dwelling on past traumas. I know, easier said than done, right? That's why I'm going to share a little secret with you— a cheat code, if you will. Make sure you have at least two or three choices in every situation. Having options is a powerful antidote to stress. Less stress equals more energy, and more energy is what leads you to that coveted state of flow.

ARE YOU POSITIVE

that you've considered the negatives?

While it's challenging to disregard the benefits of positive thinking, it's also impractical to ignore its negative aspects. Over the past decades, positive thinking has almost become a cult. It has been embraced by hordes of self-help book writers, life coaches, corporations, and influencers. I'm by no means opposed to a positive mindset - it's an incredibly effective tool for improving your life experience. However, if it's the only tool in your toolbox, you're bound to fall into the sneaky trap of blaming yourself for everything that goes wrong in your life, attributing it to your lack of a positive enough outlook.

So, let's discuss finding a balance here. Our brains aren't programmed to be constantly positive, and there's absolutely nothing wrong with that. It's simply a survival instinct that has allowed us to evolve and persevere as a species. Requiring people to completely abandon any form of negative thinking and, consequently, negative feelings is foolish, in my opinion, as it can lead to a path toward depression.

WOW!
YOU
ARE
OK!
YOU DID
GREAT!
YAY!
YOU
ROCK!

TURN YOUR INNER CRITIC

into your inner cheerleader.

That voice in your head—what does it tell you most of the time? Does it sound like your friend? Do you feel loved when you hear it? For 90 percent of people, the answer is: "Not so much."

That inner voice doesn't seem to like you at all; it notices and accentuates all the negative aspects of your personality and behavior. It feels like you're never good enough, and nothing you do is ever right. But trust me, even though you feel like it's your enemy, that inner critic has only your best interests in mind. It just doesn't know what else to focus on. Luckily, you can divert its attention to a more productive direction.

Every night, you will write down 3 reasons why you were amazing that day. You can't skip it. An answer, a reason, even if it seems very insignificant in your opinion, is required. Soon, you will notice that your inner critic is turning into your biggest fan.

BE SELFISH

and share.

Selfishness and sharing may appear contradictory, but in reality, they're not. The issue lies in the fact that we've been conditioned to believe that taking care of ourselves is synonymous with selfishness. There are so many problems, so much misery in the world! How dare you work on your own happiness! The news bombards us with horrors; media cultivates guilt over issues we often have zero power over, and as a result, we float through life—worried, low on energy, and, honestly, useless to people around us.

Let's change that. Let's be selfish and say yes to the good things in life that come our way. Let's accept them with gratitude and without guilt; let's prioritize self-care! Your interactions with people will shift into a more positive realm. You will notice that you have way more energy and a stronger desire to help people around you.

Don't be hesitant to accept help and attention from other people. We often refuse such gestures to avoid inconveniencing the ones offering, but trust me—if they are offering—it's perfectly okay to say yes! It is also absolutely fine to ask for assistance when needed.

SPREAD POSITIVITY AND GIVE THANKS

as often as you can.

The universe loves sharing and exchanging energy. However, you might notice that negative energy tends to spread and travel more swiftly. This is partially due to the fact that, as I mentioned earlier, our brains are uniquely attuned to noticing danger, causing negative information to appear more significant than positive.

That being said, negativity doesn't require your assistance to permeate the environment; positivity, on the other hand, does. Have you ever noticed that giving presents often brings more joy than receiving them? Have you ever wondered why? The act of giving and sharing something positive carries a charge that replenishes our own energy and fills us with joy.

So, start giving presents to those around you. And by presents, I mean positivity. Give praise after a positive interaction, offer compliments, and express gratitude for good service - do this both in person and online without hesitation. Did your pizza taste amazing? Leave a positive review! Was your waiter prompt? Express your thanks! Enjoyed a good cup of coffee? Share your experience with others! By doing this, you're not only helping those who have brightened your day, but you're also aiding others in discovering things and places that could improve their days.

However, don't restrict your positive responses to services alone. Look at the people around you - they are wonderful. (Even those who might not seem particularly wonderful to you possess positive qualities, I assure you!) So, tell them! Let your husband know how lucky you are to have him in your life! Tell your wife how beautiful she is! Tell your kids how talented and sweet they are! Express to your parents how much you appreciate their wisdom! Compliment a stranger on their great outfit! Do this frequently, but don't do it for the sake of receiving feedback, and don't dwell on their reactions. Allow positivity to flow, and the universe will handle the rest. Soon, you'll notice an increase in your happiness and energy levels.

The ability to understand and accept yourself is a pivotal factor in determining whether life is enjoyed or endured as a continual struggle. The initial step involves composing an honest letter to yourself about yourself - learning about who you truly are. What are your beliefs about life and self? How do you perceive your physical appearance? How do you believe others perceive you? How do you react to unexpected life events? (You'll find pages designated for this letter at the end of the journal.)

This letter is for your eyes only, so be unapologetically honest. You might discover that the tone of your letter leans more towards negativity than positivity. That's alright—this serves as the first step in getting an unfiltered glimpse of yourself, your emotions, and self-perception. Now is the time to cultivate self-kindness and acceptance. Write the same letter to your 5-year-old self. I recommend retrieving a picture or spending a few minutes crafting a mental image of yourself at that age before you begin writing. Observe how the tone of your letter differs now. Extend the same kindness and acceptance to your adult self that you were able to find for your younger version.

This kid was unique, lovable, and amazing - and these qualities are in you because you are this kid, just taller and with some emotional baggage. Start looking at yourself with loving eyes, allow yourself to make mistakes, and notice your every achievement, no matter how big or small.

. . . .

Please turn to the final pages of this journal and take a moment to compose letters to yourself.

→

11
12
1
10
2
8
4

LATER IS NOW

or never.

I know you have a list of both pleasant and necessary things that you've planned to get to later - we all do. On the following pages, jot down everything that comes to mind that you've set aside for a "better time." It's important to fill out each space.

Now, every two days, accomplish one thing from that list, even if it's just partially. Intended to write a book? Begin with the first page, at the very least! Planning to deep clean the house? Start with one room or even just your desk! Considering starting a workout routine? Start with a short morning walk! All those movies in your watch list? Watch at least one of them! Dreaming of a cross-country road trip? Drive to a neighboring town this weekend and pretend you're a tourist!

"Later" is a tremendous energy drain. Whether we consciously realize it or not, it acts like multiple open tabs on a computer, bogging down our performance. You might discover that some of the items on this list no longer resonate with you - cross them out without guilt or hesitation and enjoy the sense of relief.

TO DO LIST

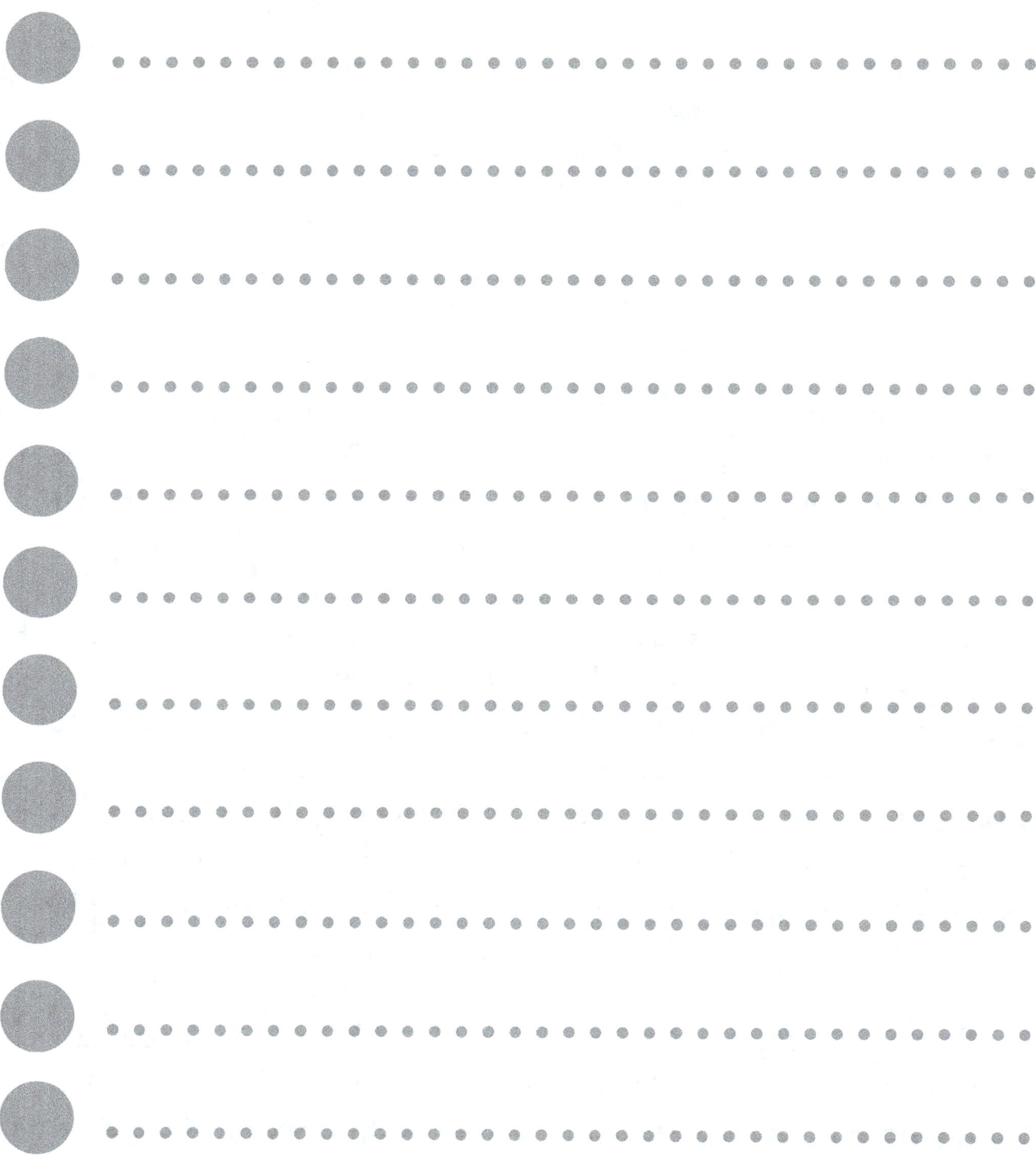

- Factor A: Personal Achievement (e.g., accomplishme
oals reached, self-esteem)
- Factor B: Social Relationships (e.g., quality of rela
ps, social support)
- Factor C: Physical Well-being (e.g., health, exercise, r
on)
- Factor D: Positive Emotio   ent,
tude)
- Factor E: Life Satisfa   sess

Assign weights to each fa   ersonal im
nce (w_A, w_B, w_C, w_D   ). These weights shoul
up to 1 (w_A + w_B + w   D   E = 1).

Evaluate each fa   from 0 to 10, wher
presents minimal s   epresents maxi
atisfaction.

Calculate th   ors:
- Happiness fr   H_A) = w_A
tor A
- Happiness fro   B) = w_B * F
or B
- Happiness from   H_C) = w_C * Fa
C
- Happiness from Posit   ions (H_D) = w_D * Fa
D
- Happiness from Life Satisfaction (H_E) = w_E * Fa

Calculate the overall happiness score (H) as the sum
dividual happiness factors:
H = H_A + H_B + H_C + H_D + H_E

THE ALGORITHM

of the universe.

We are fortunate to be living in the age of social networks because this experience makes understanding the algorithm of the universe much easier. Social media algorithms analyze your behavior and customize your feed accordingly. Liked a video with a cute puppy? Trust me, you will see more of those. Watched travel reviews? Expect more to come! The more you engage with specific content, the more of that content will populate your feed.

Interestingly enough, the universe's algorithm closely resembles the social media one. If you complain about people, brace yourself for an influx of questionable characters. Driving is bad? Expect every aspiring racing driver in the area to appear on your morning route. People are rude? Oh dear, brace yourself!

Conversely, when you start noticing the positive aspects of your life, they begin to manifest more frequently as well.

IF NOBODY IS PERFECT

then you must be nobody.

You only have one body to live your life with, and it has been doing its best to keep you going. Our world is filled with edited imagery and ever-changing trends that often make us feel dissatisfied with our appearance. Let's work on changing that.

In the following pages, you will thank your body, share how much you love it, and express your pride in it. Please, be realistic in your appreciation. Thank your body for the things you genuinely believe are positive, and don't feel compelled to thank it for things you dislike.

Self-acceptance is the first step toward loving yourself and your body, and remember that accepting yourself doesn't mean that you stop taking care of yourself and your body. Loving yourself means you are committed to making yourself healthier and happier.

33 thank-yous to your body.

My amazing body, thank you for—

1
2
3
4
5
6
7
8
9
10
11
12
13
14
15
16

17
18
19
20
21
22
23
24
25
26
27
28
29
30
31
32
33

HOW TO

Today I'm grateful for-

What are you grateful for today? One or two things should suffice.

Because -

Explain why you are grateful for them, and try to look beyond the obvious reasons if you can.

What made me amazing today?

Write about something you did or didn't do, felt or didn't feel today that deserves praise. It doesn't matter how big or small in your opinion. Saved the world? You are amazing! Didn't kill the spider? You are amazing! Cleaned your room? Well, you get the idea!

Tomorrow I plan to make myself happy by-

Every day, you should plan to do something to make yourself happy the following day, even if it's just for 10-15 minutes - take a stroll, listen to music, treat yourself, watch your favorite show, meditate, or simply do nothing without feeling guilty about it.

DATE _______________ S M T W T F S

Today I'm grateful for-

____

____

____

Because -

____

____

____

What made me amazing today?

____

____

Tomorrow I plan to make myself happy by-

____

____

____

DATE ______________   S M T W T F S

Today I'm grateful for—

____

____

____

Because —

____

____

____

What made me amazing today?

____

____

Tomorrow I plan to make myself happy by—

____

____

____

DATE _______________ S M T W T F S

Today I'm grateful for-

____

____

____

Because -

____

____

____

What made me amazing today?

____

____

Tomorrow I plan to make myself happy by-

____

____

____

DATE _______________   S M T W T F S

Today I'm grateful for-

____

____

____

Because -

____

____

____

What made me amazing today?

____

____

Tomorrow I plan to make myself happy by-

____

____

____

DATE

S M T W T F S

Today I'm grateful for-

____

____

____

Because -

____

____

____

What made me amazing today?

____

____

Tomorrow I plan to make myself happy by-

____

____

____

S M T W T F S

Today I'm grateful for-

____

____

____

Because -

____

____

____

What made me amazing today?

____

____

Tomorrow I plan to make myself happy by-

____

____

DATE _______________ S M T W T F S

Today I'm grateful for-

____

____

____

Because -

____

____

____

What made me amazing today?

____

____

Tomorrow I plan to make myself happy by-

____

____

____

S M T W T F S

Today I'm grateful for-

____

____

____

Because -

____

____

____

What made me amazing Today?

____

____

____

Tomorrow I plan to make myself happy by-

____

____

____

DATE

S M T W T F S

Today I'm grateful for-

Because -

What made me amazing today?

Tomorrow I plan to make myself happy by-

DATE
S M T W T F S
Today I'm grateful for-
Because -
What made me amazing today?
Tomorrow I plan to make myself happy by-

Today I'm grateful for-

____

____

____

Because -

____

____

____

What made me amazing today?

____

____

Tomorrow I plan to make myself happy by-

____

____

____

DATE ________________   S M T W T F S

Today I'm grateful for-

Because -

What made me amazing today?

Tomorrow I plan to make myself happy by-

DATE

S M T W T F S

Today I'm grateful for-

Because -

What made me amazing today?

Tomorrow I plan to make myself happy by-

DATE _______________ S M T W T F S

Today I'm grateful for-

____

____

____

Because -

____

____

____

What made me amazing Today?

____

____

____

Tomorrow I plan to make myself happy by-

____

____

____

DATE ______________   S M T W T F S

Today I'm grateful for-

____

____

____

Because -

____

____

____

What made me amazing Today?

____

____

____

Tomorrow I plan to make myself happy by-

____

____

____

S M T W T F S

Today I'm grateful for-

____

____

____

Because -

____

____

____

What made me amazing today?

____

____

Tomorrow I plan to make myself happy by-

____

____

____

DATE

S M T W T F S

Today I'm grateful for-

Because -

What made me amazing today?

Tomorrow I plan to make myself happy by-

S M T W T F S

Today I'm grateful for-

____

____

____

Because -

____

____

____

What made me amazing today?

____

____

Tomorrow I plan to make myself happy by-

____

____

____

Today I'm grateful for-

____

____

____

Because -

____

____

____

What made me amazing today?

____

____

Tomorrow I plan to make myself happy by-

____

____

____

DATE

S M T W T F S

Today I'm grateful for-

Because -

What made me amazing today?

Tomorrow I plan to make myself happy by-

DATE
S M T W T F S
Today I'm grateful for-
Because -
What made me amazing today?
Tomorrow I plan to make myself happy by-

DATE S M T W T F S

Today I'm grateful for-

____

____

____

Because -

____

____

____

What made me amazing Today?

____

____

____

Tomorrow I plan to make myself happy by-

____

____

____

Today I'm grateful for-

____
____
____

Because -

____
____
____

What made me amazing today?

____
____

Tomorrow I plan to make myself happy by-

____
____
____

DATE _______________ S M T W T F S

Today I'm grateful for-

____

____

____

Because -

____

____

____

What made me amazing today?

____

____

Tomorrow I plan to make myself happy by-

____

____

____

DATE

S M T W T F S

Today I'm grateful for-

____

____

____

Because -

____

____

____

What made me amazing today?

____

____

Tomorrow I plan to make myself happy by-

____

____

____

DATE
S M T W T F S
Today I'm grateful for-
Because -
What made me amazing today?
Tomorrow I plan to make myself happy by-

DATE _______________ S M T W T F S

Today I'm grateful for-

____

____

____

Because -

____

____

____

What made me amazing today?

____

____

Tomorrow I plan to make myself happy by-

____

____

DATE ________________   S M T W T F S

Today I'm grateful for-

____

____

____

Because -

____

____

____

What made me amazing today?

____

____

Tomorrow I plan to make myself happy by-

____

____

____

DATE
S M T W T F S
Today I'm grateful for-
Because -
What made me amazing today?
Tomorrow I plan to make myself happy by-

DATE ___________
S M T W T F S
Today I'm grateful for-
Because -
What made me amazing today?
Tomorrow I plan to make myself happy by-

DATE _______________   S M T W T F S

Today I'm grateful for-

____

____

____

Because -

____

____

____

What made me amazing today?

____

____

____

Tomorrow I plan to make myself happy by-

____

____

____

DATE

S M T W T F S

Today I'm grateful for-

Because -

What made me amazing today?

Tomorrow I plan to make myself happy by-

DATE ______________   S M T W T F S

____

____

____

____

____

____

____

____

____

____

____

DATE ______________   S M T W T F S

Today I'm grateful for-

Because -

What made me amazing today?

Tomorrow I plan to make myself happy by-

S M T W T F S

Today I'm grateful for-

Because -

What made me amazing today?

Tomorrow I plan to make myself happy by-

Today I'm grateful for-

____

____

____

Because -

____

____

____

What made me amazing today?

____

____

Tomorrow I plan to make myself happy by-

____

____

____

DATE _______________   S M T W T F S

Today I'm grateful for-

____

____

____

Because -

____

____

____

What made me amazing today?

____

____

____

Tomorrow I plan to make myself happy by-

____

____

____

DATE _______________   S M T W T F S

Today I'm grateful for-

____

____

____

Because -

____

____

____

What made me amazing today?

____

____

____

Tomorrow I plan to make myself happy by-

____

____

____

DATE _______________   S M T W T F S

Today I'm grateful for-

____

____

____

Because -

____

____

____

What made me amazing today?

____

____

Tomorrow I plan to make myself happy by-

____

____

Today I'm grateful for-

____
____
____

Because -

____
____
____

What made me amazing today?

____
____
____

Tomorrow I plan to make myself happy by-

____
____
____

DATE

S M T W T F S

Today I'm grateful for-

Because -

What made me amazing today?

Tomorrow I plan to make myself happy by-

DATE

S M T W T F S

Today I'm grateful for-

Because -

What made me amazing today?

Tomorrow I plan to make myself happy by-

DATE _______________ S M T W T F S

Today I'm grateful for-

____

____

____

Because -

____

____

____

What made me amazing today?

____

____

Tomorrow I plan to make myself happy by-

____

____

____

Today I'm grateful for-

____

____

____

____

Because -

____

____

____

What made me amazing today?

____

____

Tomorrow I plan to make myself happy by-

____

____

____

Today I'm grateful for-

Because -

What made me amazing today?

Tomorrow I plan to make myself happy by-

DATE _______________ S M T W T F S

Today I'm grateful for-

____

____

____

Because -

____

____

____

What made me amazing Today?

____

____

Tomorrow I plan to make myself happy by-

____

____

____

DATE

S M T W T F S

Today I'm grateful for-

____

____

____

____

Because -

____

____

____

____

What made me amazing today?

____

____

____

Tomorrow I plan to make myself happy by-

____

____

____

Today I'm grateful for-

Because -

What made me amazing today?

Tomorrow I plan to make myself happy by-

Today I'm grateful for-

____
____
____

Because -

____
____
____

What made me amazing today?

____
____

Tomorrow I plan to make myself happy by-

____
____

DATE S M T W T F S

Today I'm grateful for-

____

____

____

____

Because -

____

____

____

What made me amazing today?

____

____

____

Tomorrow I plan to make myself happy by-

____

____

____

DATE
S M T W T F S

Today I'm grateful for-

Because -

What made me amazing today?

Tomorrow I plan to make myself happy by-

DATE ______________   S M T W T F S

Today I'm grateful for-

____

____

____

____

Because -

____

____

____

What made me amazing today?

____

____

____

Tomorrow I plan to make myself happy by-

____

____

____

DATE

S M T W T F S

Today I'm grateful for-

Because -

What made me amazing today?

Tomorrow I plan to make myself happy by-

DATE ___________   S M T W T F S

Today I'm grateful for-

____
____
____

Because -

____
____
____

What made me amazing Today?

____
____

Tomorrow I plan to make myself happy by-

____
____
____

                          S   M   T   W   T   F   S

Today I'm grateful for-

____

____

____

Because -

____

____

____

What made me amazing today?

____

____

Tomorrow I plan to make myself happy by-

____

____

____

Today I'm grateful for-

____

____

____

Because -

____

____

____

What made me amazing today?

____

____

Tomorrow I plan to make myself happy by-

____

____

____

DATE _______________   S M T W T F S

Today I'm grateful for-

____
____
____

Because -

____
____
____

What made me amazing today?

____
____

Tomorrow I plan to make myself happy by-

____
____
____

DATE _________________   S M T W T F S

Today I'm grateful for-

____
____
____

Because -

____
____
____

What made me amazing today?

____
____

Tomorrow I plan to make myself happy by-

____
____
____

Today I'm grateful for-

____

____

____

Because -

____

____

____

What made me amazing today?

____

____

Tomorrow I plan to make myself happy by-

____

____

____

DATE
S M T W T F S
Today I'm grateful for-

Because -

What made me amazing today?

Tomorrow I plan to make myself happy by-

Today I'm grateful for-

Because -

What made me amazing today?

Tomorrow I plan to make myself happy by-

DATE

S M T W T F S

Today I'm grateful for-

Because -

What made me amazing today?

Tomorrow I plan to make myself happy by-

DATE _______________ S M T W T F S

Today I'm grateful for-

____

____

____

Because -

____

____

____

What made me amazing today?

____

____

Tomorrow I plan to make myself happy by-

____

____

____

DATE _______________ S M T W T F S

Today I'm grateful for-

____
____
____

Because -

____
____
____

What made me amazing today?

____
____

Tomorrow I plan to make myself happy by-

____
____

Today I'm grateful for-

Because -

What made me amazing today?

Tomorrow I plan to make myself happy by-

DATE _______________   S M T W T F S

Today I'm grateful for-

____
____
____
____

Because -

____
____
____

What made me amazing today?

____
____
____

Tomorrow I plan to make myself happy by-

____
____
____

Today I'm grateful for-

Because -

What made me amazing today?

Tomorrow I plan to make myself happy by-

DATE
S M T W T F S
Today I'm grateful for-
Because -
What made me amazing today?
Tomorrow I plan to make myself happy by-

DATE

S M T W T F S

Today I'm grateful for-

Because -

What made me amazing today?

Tomorrow I plan to make myself happy by-

DATE _______________   S M T W T F S

Today I'm grateful for-

____

____

____

Because -

____

____

____

What made me amazing Today?

____

____

____

Tomorrow I plan to make myself happy by-

____

____

____

DATE _____________ S M T W T F S

Today I'm grateful for-

____

____

____

Because -

____

____

____

What made me amazing today?

____

____

Tomorrow I plan to make myself happy by-

____

____

____

Today I'm grateful for-

Because -

What made me amazing today?

Tomorrow I plan to make myself happy by-

Today I'm grateful for-

Because -

What made me amazing today?

Tomorrow I plan to make myself happy by-

DATE _______   S M T W T F S

Today I'm grateful for-

____

____

____

Because -

____

____

____

What made me amazing today?

____

____

Tomorrow I plan to make myself happy by-

____

____

____

DATE

S M T W T F S

Today I'm grateful for-

Because -

What made me amazing today?

Tomorrow I plan to make myself happy by-

DATE
S M T W T F S
Today I'm grateful for-

Because -

What made me amazing today?

Tomorrow I plan to make myself happy by-

DATE
S M T W T F S

Today I'm grateful for-

Because -

What made me amazing today?

Tomorrow I plan to make myself happy by-

DATE S M T W T F S

Today I'm grateful for—

____

____

____

Because —

____

____

____

What made me amazing today?

____

____

____

Tomorrow I plan to make myself happy by—

____

____

____

DATE _______________   S M T W T F S

Today I'm grateful for-

____
____
____
____

Because -

____
____
____

What made me amazing today?

____
____

Tomorrow I plan to make myself happy by-

____
____
____

Today I'm grateful for-

____

____

____

____

Because -

____

____

____

What made me amazing today?

____

____

Tomorrow I plan to make myself happy by-

____

____

____

DATE _______________ S M T W T F S

Today I'm grateful for-

____

____

____

Because -

____

____

____

What made me amazing today?

____

____

Tomorrow I plan to make myself happy by-

____

____

____

DATE ______________   S M T W T F S

Today I'm grateful for-

____

____

____

Because -

____

____

____

What made me amazing today?

____

____

____

Tomorrow I plan to make myself happy by-

____

____

____

DATE _______________   S M T W T F S

Today I'm grateful for-

____

____

____

Because -

____

____

____

What made me amazing today?

____

____

Tomorrow I plan to make myself happy by-

____

____

____

DATE

S M T W T F S

Today I'm grateful for-

Because -

What made me amazing today?

Tomorrow I plan to make myself happy by-

DATE _______________   S M T W T F S

Today I'm grateful for-

____

____

____

Because -

____

____

____

What made me amazing today?

____

____

Tomorrow I plan to make myself happy by-

____

____

____

DATE S M T W T F S

Today I'm grateful for-

____

____

____

Because -

____

____

____

What made me amazing today?

____

____

Tomorrow I plan to make myself happy by-

____

____

____

DATE _______________ S M T W T F S

Today I'm grateful for-

____

____

____

Because -

____

____

____

What made me amazing today?

____

____

Tomorrow I plan to make myself happy by-

____

____

____

DATE _______________ S M T W T F S

Today I'm grateful for-

____

____

____

Because -

____

____

____

What made me amazing today?

____

____

Tomorrow I plan to make myself happy by-

____

____

DATE
S M T W T F S

Today I'm grateful for-

Because -

What made me amazing today?

Tomorrow I plan to make myself happy by-

S M T W T F S

Today I'm grateful for-

Because -

What made me amazing Today?

Tomorrow I plan to make myself happy by-

DATE _______________ S M T W T F S

Today I'm grateful for-

____

____

____

Because -

____

____

____

What made me amazing today?

____

____

Tomorrow I plan to make myself happy by-

____

____

____

DATE

S M T W T F S

Today I'm grateful for-

Because -

What made me amazing today?

Tomorrow I plan to make myself happy by-

DATE

S M T W T F S

Today I'm grateful for-

Because -

What made me amazing today?

Tomorrow I plan to make myself happy by-

LETTERS TO YOURSELF

DEAR ME...

DEAR FIVE-YEAR-OLD ME...

I hope these three months have helped you see your life from a more positive perspective. You've started to trust yourself and the universe a bit more, and you've learned to love yourself just for being you!

www.ingramcontent.com/pod-product-compliance
Lightning Source LLC
Chambersburg PA
CBHW082019150726
48196CB00073B/550